The Cheat Code

How to Successfully Complete Probation and Parole

Jonas Royster & Armand King

For permissions contact:
paradisepublishingcompany@gmail.com
Jonas Royster
30450 Haun Road #1041
Menifee, CA 92584
jonasroyster@hoodproverbz.com
www.hoodproverbz.com

Printed Worldwide
First Printing 2024
First Edition 2024
ISBN: 979-8-9887279-3-4

Co-Published by Paradise Publishing Company and Walk With Me Impact
Media & Education

Table of Contents

A Message to the Homies and the Homegirls

What it do luv ones!

If you're reading this, it's because you are either finna touchdown or you have just gotten out. Whatever the case, I want to congratulate you. *Why?* you might ask. Because you're taking time to run through this booklet. You and I both know that time is the most valuable commodity, so much so that no matter how much money you get, you can never buy any time back. So, thank you for spending your time with my potna and I—we definitely appreciate it.

Let's talk a little bit about me and my potna, who co-authored this book. We have both been behind them walls. I've done state, and he's done fed time, so when it comes to discharging a number or what they like to say, "successfully complete probation or parole," we both done it, and we both haven't caught a new one in over a decade. To us, that's what successfully completing probation and parole is all about. It's not just about getting off paperwork—it's about never getting back on it. Recidivism is a real thing. If you don't know what that means, it means catching another case and getting locked back up.

For the record, the recidivism rate in America is real, and it is outrageous. The *Harvard Political Review* released an article on August 8th, 2021, stating that "each year, more than 600,000 individuals are released from state and federal prisons. Another 9 million were released from local jails within three years of their release, two of three former prisoners were rearrested, and more than 50% are incarcerated again." So, America's recidivism rate is 76.6% of prisoners are rearrested within five years. That's why getting out is important, but staying out is the key to freedom in life.

In this short booklet, we are gonna share with you some steps and tips to get you off paperwork and help you beat the recidivism "trap." These steps are things that have helped us and other homies and homegirls who have successfully completed probation or parole and have stayed out for good. Also, know this—this ain't the end all be all. This is not the only way you can successfully complete probation and parole; however, this is a guide for you to reference as you're on the journey to living the life you choose to create. Thank you for trusting us while you successfully complete probation and parole and staying out for good.

Much Luv 2 our luv 1s,
Royster & Armand King

STEPS

"Life's a test, mistakes are lessons, but the gift of life is knowing that you have made a difference."

– Nas

STEP 1: Change Your Mind, Change Your Results

(It's you vs you)

This step right here may not seem like much, but it's the key to unlocking every door you ever want to open. Changing how we think ultimately changes our behaviors and our actions. As you read in the letter, our thoughts and goals must change from "I'm getting out" to "I'm getting out, and I'm staying out for good." These two statements are two totally different mindsets. Let me explain.

The mind is a cold piece of work. We can lead it down any road we want simply with our thoughts and how we phrase sentences, statements, and questions. Check this example out and repeat this statement to yourself. "It's hard to succeed when you have a felony on your record."

Where did your mind take you after you said that? I know where mine went—it began to validate that statement. My mind began to replay all the times I had ever said that phrase, and then I started to agree with it. That's called "confirmation bias." In simple words, confirmation bias is when our brain acts like a detective that's only looking for clues to prove what we already believe instead of looking at all the evidence, both for and against our beliefs.

Now repeat this to yourself and do the same process: "What do I need right now to succeed when I get out?" Your mind did the same thing as it did with the first statement. It went down a path to get you answers or agree with it. You probably started to rattle off a handful of things you know you need once you touch down. This is how our mind works, y'all.

So, let's revisit these statements: "I'm getting out," and "I'm getting out, and this time I'm staying out." For me, "I'm getting out" leads my mind to think about doing all the "fun" things I felt like I missed out on while I was down. Now, when I say to myself the other statement, "I'm getting out, and I'm staying out for good." My mind started to spotlight all the things I must avoid, and it gave me ideas on what I thought it would take to stay out for good. Believe me, your mind will do the same.

When changing our minds, we must also change who we believe is responsible for us to complete probation and parole successfully and stay out for good. Let me tell you this: it ain't your probation or parole officer, it ain't your girl or your man, your husband or your wife, your momma or daddy, your granny or your auntie. The only person responsible for getting you off paperwork is you! It will always be only you—no one else. You must take extreme ownership of this responsibility.

What does taking extreme ownership mean? If we are supposed to see our probation or parole officer next Thursday, and the ride we lined up suddenly can't take us any more, then you find another solution to get there. We call someone else, hit the bus, and walk if we can, but whatever we do, we must take ownership of our responsibility. It ain't no one's job or obligation to take us. We da'one who got locked up, not them. So, let's not start pointing fingers and blaming them because when we do, we once again take a back seat in our own lives. Remember, staying out is about us taking our power back and taking extreme ownership in all our decisions, plans, and choices. When we do that, we can live a life of true freedom—a life without ever getting locked up again.

"Every day is a new opportunity to change your life and be who you want to be."

– Tupac Shakur

STEP 2: Proper Preparation Prevents Poor Performance

(Create a plan for success)

Now that we are getting a grip on how important it is to change our mindset and the fact that what we think dictates our results, the next step is to create a plan for success. One day, I heard someone recite a quote by Confucious: "A man shoots at nothing, sure to hit it." I ain't gonna lie; it sounded dope when he said it, but I still didn't get it. So I asked him, "What does it mean?" He took the toothpick from the corner of his mouth and looked over my head like he was staring at some whimsical wizard giving him the answers. "It means a man is always aiming. Some aim at something while others aim at nothing, but you always hit what you aim at." The question you should begin to ask yourself is, "What am I aiming at?" My hope for you is that your answer is "getting off paperwork and staying out forever."

Now, now, now, everyone. I know to some of you that the forever part sounds straight-up ridiculous, but let me tell you, it's hella doable once you take the time to set up a plan. The advantage of creating a plan is for us not to have to wing it when shit hits the fan. A plan can help you get back on track when you fall off course. When you have a written plan, you can always go back and see where things started to get off track. A plan is a set of instructions that will get you to your end goal, sort of like an instructional manual when building a bike. If you have a couple of bolts and nuts left over when you're done, you can go back to the instructional manual (plan) and see where you got off track, then identify the issue and adjust so you can get back on track.

Now that we know why a plan can set us up for success and keep us on track, it's time to identify what to plan for. Here's a list of things I remember planning for when I was finna touchdown. First, where would I rest my head when I returned home? At the time I was paroled, I was homeless. I couldn't stay with my pops. My moms had remarried, and her husband told her that I couldn't stay with them. I didn't have a girlfriend at the time, nor did I have any other family, and I damn sure wasn't finna stay at any of my homies' pads and bring the police over there. So, I was homeless. I knew I must create a plan to put a roof over my head.

For me, at that time, the plan was to get a housing voucher from my parole officer when I touched down and live there for as long as I could until I could get a job and stack my money so I could either get my own place or rent a room somewhere. Although the housing facility I stayed at felt like I was locked up all over again, and, truth be told, I hated it. I was willing to sacrifice that feeling of hate and confinement for the bigger goal of staying out forever. I knew if I didn't follow through with this plan, I would catch a violation for absconding, and that would send me right back to where I didn't want to be.

What are some of the things you have to plan for? Is it finding a place to rest your head, getting an ID, driver's license, birth certificate, or social security card? What about finding a job, returning to school to get your GED or high school diploma, or even going to college? You may need to create a plan on how to find and get custody of your child or children. Remember, the first thing we should do is identify what we want (our end goal) and then take aim at it. When we do that, we then start taking steps. Small or big. It doesn't matter because all our steps will add up to great distances over time.

"Stay far from timid.
Only make moves when
your heart's in it, and
live the phrase 'Sky's
the limit."
– The Notorious B.I.G.

STEP 3: Bad Association Prevents from Being Enormous

(Choosing the right company)

Choosing the right company to be around once we touchdown can be the most challenging step out of all the steps. Why? Because for most of us, the company we're around, we consider family, although we now know they might not be the best influence on us. How challenging is it to not see your brother, sister, uncle, auntie, mom, or pops? That's a hard pill to swallow. Especially if you are like me and you don't have much blood-related family. Friends and homies become your family; not seeing them or hanging out with them feels like torture.

To keep it a buck with y'all, before I knew how to complete probation and parole and stay out for good, I caught multiple violations for what they called "being around documented gang members." I labeled them family, but to my probation and parole officers, that didn't matter. The bottom line was I wasn't supposed to be around them. The result of that was a probation violation that got me six months back in the county, and I violated again when I was on parole back in 2007, and that was twelve flat back in the pen. In that last violation for me back in 2007, I vowed to myself I would never do this shit again. Although I love my homies (my brothers and sisters, aunties, and uncles), six to twelve months back behind the wall just wasn't worth it.

To complete this step, you're gonna have to give up things that feel good (hanging with certain friends, homies, and family members) for what will feel great in the future (not violating, discharging your number, getting off paperwork, and never getting locked back up). Giving something up now for a greater future is labeled a sacrifice. If you think you can't do it, let me tell you that you can because we all sacrifice daily. You're sacrificing your time right now as you read this booklet so that in the future, you have the steps for getting off paperwork and staying out for good. Look at it this way. You sacrificed your freedom for whatever you wanted to do that got you behind the wall. We sacrifice things all the time, mainly for the things we want now, but successful people tend to sacrifice what they want now for the big thing they are going after in the future. What are you willing to sacrifice to complete probation or parole and never come back?

Take a couple of minutes to really put some thought into that. Let that question fester in your mind. I ain't saying you ain't got to be around them ever again, but I am suggesting that you don't be around them right now. Remember, those people you are sacrificing your freedom to be around weren't with you when you were locked up, so putting them on ice for another six months to a couple of years until you get off paperwork ain't finna hurt nobody.

"If you look at the people in your circle and don't get inspired, then you don't have a circle. You have a cage."

– Nipsey Hussle

STEP 4: The Don't Know's Won't Know So Make Sure You Know

(Ignorance is not bliss)

Have you ever been with someone, whether it was your homie, sibling, or even an associate, and they took you somewhere different than where you thought you were supposed to be going? How about once you all got there, they did something you had no clue they were going to do, like stopping to bust a tip at some random house along the way or going to the liquor store in a neighborhood that you probably don't want to be in and them taking off on someone? Or maybe they took you to their girlfriend's or boyfriend's house. They got into a big fight, and the police came. Meanwhile, you're sitting in the car the whole time, asking yourself *What the hell is happening? I ain't sign up for this shit.*

News flash—you did. Why do I say that? It's because you chose not knowing to care over caring to know. Now, don't get me wrong, you could've asked some questions, and they may have even lied and told you they were finna take you exactly where you asked them to take you, and then all of a sudden, they did what they did—but remember you are ultimately responsible for the choices and decisions you make, not anyone else. You didn't have to ask them; you chose to ask them. It may have been a last option, but the keyword there is that it was still an option.

When we choose not knowing to care, what that means is that we secretly want to be able to use that as an excuse later if something goes wrong. I remember I was on my way to a meeting with a gentleman I highly respected, and by the time I arrived, I was six minutes late. As I opened his door, the first thing I said was, "My bad for my tardiness, but there was a little bit of traffic when I exited." He looked at me without even batting an eye and said, "Excuses only sound good to the one who is saying it." Then he excused me from his office and told me to return next week.

When we are on the journey toward completing probation or parole and staying out for good, making excuses on why we don't know something regarding our stipulations and conditions is like walking on a tightrope suspended across the Grand Canyon without any support or a net at the bottom. It's outright ridiculous! Now, could it be done? Yes, but how many of us are willing to take that risk? If you agree you wouldn't take the gamble of walking that tightrope, then we must not walk the tightrope of being on paperwork. To stay out for good and complete probation or parole, those risks are unnecessary. All we must do is begin asking questions.

Asking questions to your P.O. to get a better understanding and more clarity on your stipulations and conditions is paramount to completion. If you have a stipulation that says no contact with any of your co-defendants, as I had, but one of your co-defendants is a family member, before you go and hang with them, I suggest you take the extra precautions and run it by your P.O. first. All they can say is "yes" or "no." However, at least you have the information to make a well-informed choice.

Take this scenario. What if you are a documented gang member and you have an uncle who is as well? He stays with granny, and when you get out, you're going to stay at granny's house too. You know one of your stipulations is not to be around any documented gang members. There are two ways to play this. The first one, which most of us do, is act like we don't care and deal with whatever the consequences are if we get caught. The second way to play this is to be responsible and holla at your P.O. and let them know the scenario. It can be as simple as this: "I know I ain't supposed to be hanging out with documented gang members, but I have family who is, and we all stay under the same roof. Will you violate me if you come for a visit and we're all in the house at the same time?"

Best believe they are gonna give you an answer. Some may not trip. I've had some P.O.'s that kept it a hunnid with me and said, "I not worried about you all being at the same house at the same time, but if you get caught outside those walls together, I'm violating you." Then you have others who are by the book who may say, "I don't care who they are. You better find yourself another place to live and not get caught with them."

Whether it sounds unfair or not, the point is we've asked the questions, so now we know the expectations and the repercussions. Let me tell you this: ignorance is not bliss. Ignorance is not an excuse. Ignorance can cost you a violation or even a new case. Don't be the don't know, be the one who knows, so you can be the one who stays out for good and completes probation and parole successfully.

"I've got to do what's right for me and not live my life the way anybody else wants it."
— 50 Cent

STEP 5: "No" Ain't a Bad Word—Don't Be Scared to Use It

(Use it often and without regret)

I know you're probably like, "No shit. I know 'no' ain't a bad word." Well, if you know that, I suggest you begin to learn how to use it more often. "No" is an interesting word because it can be understood in many languages. "No" is a universal word, yet some people, when the word "no" is said to them, act as if they've just been cussed at or slapped in the face.

Has any family member, someone you're cool with, or even someone you're dating asked you for your time, money, advice, or a huge favor, and you finally said "no" to them? Don't they act like, "How dare you say 'no' to me?" That's because, to some people, the word "no" is like hearing "f*ck you." Now, most of us ain't into cursing out our friends, family, or loved ones, but because we've always said "yes" to these people, that's how it's often perceived.

For most of us who've been on this merry-go-round of getting locked up and getting out, then getting locked back up again, there is another person we hardly say "no" to, and that's ourselves. Think about it. There are many times in your life that you know the right thing to do is to say "no" to yourself, but you end up shrugging that "no" off, and the next thing you know, you are doing that thing you told yourself you were gonna quit once you were released. Or even better yet, that you told yourself you'll never do again.

For your boy, that "no" I kept ignoring was the "no" to my drinking and drugging, and I ain't talking about smoking weed. Most times, when I had the urge to drink, pop a pill, or do any other drug, I would initially say "no" to myself, then that little whisper voice in my head would say, "It's a'ight. You can gon' ahead and do it today and stop tomorrow. You've been doing good. One time ain't gon' matter."

When you are on your path to completing probation or parole and staying out for good, that last whisper of "You've been doing good, one time ain't gon' matter" is one of the biggest detractors that can put you on a fast track to a violation or new beef. When you hear that whisper, you must say "no" to it. To this day, I even say "no" out loud to hear myself say it. It helps to draw a distinction between the whispering voice in my head and the real me, and it helps keep me accountable to myself.

Now, I do know this is not an easy task, especially if you've been a person who has been saying yes to others and yourself for over the last three years. Give yourself some grace and be patient because it ain't gonna change overnight. For some "no's," it may take one week of constantly saying it; for others, you may need to say "no" to the same thing for one year. However, to see long-lasting results, that's what's needed to complete probation or parole and successfully stay out for good. Also, remember this: "no" is not a bad word, and you may have to tell yourself and others that simple yet harsh two-letter word more than once so that you and they begin to believe it.

"If you look at the people in your circle and don't get inspired, then you don't have a circle. You have a cage."

— Nipsey Hussle

STEP 6: Idle Time is the Devil's Playground

(Positive production throughout the day is your antidote)

I remember hearing this step's title for the first time in the summer of 2002. At that time, I was on probation, and I was at one of my regular monthly visits with my probation officer so I could drop it in the bottle. He asked me all the questions a probation officer typically asks when you haven't seen him in a month. As I'm sitting on the hard black plastic fold-out chair tap dancing around his questions, he hits me with this one, "Mr. Royster, do you have a job yet?"

My chest expanded like I was blowing up a balloon at a five-year-old's birthday party, and then, it instantly retracted. The answers that were so smoothly flowing out of my mouth before now fumbled, and the most commonly used answer spilled out, "I've been filling out applications, but ain't no one hiring me."

My probation officer picked up the generic coffee mug from the center of his desk, pressed it to his lips, and took a long sip. His eyes attempted to pierce my soul, but there wasn't much left in there at the time. "Look, Mr. Royster, I ain't stupid. You know how many times I've heard that bullshit before from someone sitting in that exact same chair?" My shoulders raised, then dropped. "Thousands of times, young man. If you have nothing positive to occupy your time, your time will occupy you. Remember, idle time is the devil's playground."

Sitting there, he continued to tell me some other things, but I'd already checked out. I was ready to get back to them streets and do what I was doing. It wasn't until about six years later that I truly understood what he said to me. If we have too much free time on our hands and when we ain't got anything positive and productive going on in our days, we

29

typically go back to our old habits, which can lead us behind them bars.

Think about this: when you touch down, if you're not using most of your day to take care of business like getting an ID, driver's license, social security card, or birth certificate, looking for a place to stay, looking for a job, or going to school, then you are gonna have a gang of time on your hands to do a whole bunch of nothing. When we ain't doing nothing, you and I know we're really doing something, and that something most likely is not gonna help us complete probation and parole and stay out for good.

One of the best things for me that kept me from catching another violation and finally successfully completing parole and keeping my butt out for good was getting a job that demanded most of my time. I even worked on weekends and holidays. That was key for me to beat the "trap" of recidivism. Why? Because it kept me away from the bullshit in the streets without me even realizing it at first. It kept my time occupied enough with something productive, which gave me no time for devilish thoughts and turning them devilish thoughts into actions.

Remember, your time is yours to do what you want with, but if you choose to do nothing with it, best believe there is someone who is waiting to help you with that time, and let me tell you, it most likely ain't God. Find something productive and positive to do with your time, something that will help you avoid and miss the bullshit that's waiting for you.

"Anything's possible,
you gotta dream like
you never seen
obstacles."
– J. Cole

STEP 7: Your Success is in Your Routine

(Small steps, great distances)

Completing probation or parole successfully and staying out for good is simply about creating good routines for yourself. Some might not like the word I'm about to say, but for others, it may mean everything to you: "programming." We've all heard this word before, and all programming is, essentially, a routine. To simplify it, when we run a clean or smooth program, we get better results.

By definition, a program is a set of related measures or activities with a particular long-term aim. The long-term aim is to complete probation and parole and stay out for good successfully. By implementing the previous six steps, you will begin to create a routine for yourself that you can measure daily on your way to getting off paperwork and staying from behind them walls for good.

Check it out. I know for some of y'all, this may sound like some fluff, some cap, maybe even some bullshit, but at the end of the day, this will work *if* you work it! Nothing worth having in life is handed to us on a silver platter. If we want it, then we have to go after it. We can't let our excuses or past failures make us believe that we can't get it done. We can. Just because we made stupid choices in our lives doesn't mean we're stupid. It means we made a choice to risk our freedom, and now I'm asking you to make a choice to protect it. We're not saying it's going to be easy, but we are saying that it will be worth it.

You are worth every bit of it. You have greatness within, but it's up to you to look for it, find it, and refine it. This is why you have been given the opportunity to hit these streets again. Your time is now; you may stumble and even fall along this journey, but we urge you never to quit, never to lay on your back and stay there. If you fall seven times, get up eight. Remember, quitters never win, and winners never quit. Which one are you?

We wish you all the best as you take this journey toward staying on the outside of them walls forever. From us to you, just know it's all love, and we wish you the best in every way possible. If you need to holla at us, then get with us. Find us on social media and DM us or get our info from the back of the book. We are here for you. Much luv, luv ones!

TIPS

"Sometimes, it's the journey that teaches you a lot about your destination."
– Drake

TIP 1: Focusing on Self-Improvement During Probation

Prioritize Personal Growth Over Relationships

If you're currently not in a relationship, it's a good time to focus solely on yourself. Concentrate on building your character, improving your education, and finding a job. These efforts will put you in a better position for the future and prevent you from ending up in difficult situations again. Remember, when you work on being the best version of yourself, the right people will naturally be drawn to your life.

The Benefits of "Dating Yourself"

I understand the natural human desire to be in a relationship, but if you can put that aside for now and focus on self-improvement, it will be beneficial. By concentrating on getting through your probation and bettering yourself, you'll be in a much stronger position later.

If You're Already in a Supportive Relationship

If you're already in a relationship that's supportive, helps you grow, and aids you in successfully completing probation, then it's okay to stay in that relationship. However, if you find yourself entering a new relationship while on probation and parole, ensure it is one that genuinely supports your journey to completion. If not, it's better to wait and focus on yourself.

The Risks of Chasing Relationships

Seeking a relationship during this time can lead to making poor choices. It might involve going to places you should avoid, staying out late, or even engaging in illegal activities to impress or support the other person. These actions could endanger your freedom. Instead of chasing a relationship, invest that energy in improving yourself and advancing to the next level.

The Bottom Line: Self-Improvement First

The period of probation and parole is a critical time for self-improvement. Focusing on your own growth helps you successfully complete probation and parole and prepares you for healthier relationships in the future. Build a solid foundation for yourself first; everything else will follow in due course.

"You can want success all you want, but to get it, you can't falter. You can't slip. You can't sleep. One eye open, for real, and forever."

– Jay-Z

TIP 2: Create Your Plan for Success

Identify Your End Goal

Clearly define what you want to achieve. Whether it's staying out of jail, securing a job, or furthering your education, knowing your end goal gives you something concrete to aim for.

Create a Detailed Plan

Just like an instruction manual helps you assemble a bike, a well-thought-out plan guides you toward your goal. This could include steps for finding housing, obtaining necessary documents like an ID or driver's license, or strategies for job hunting or education.

Be Prepared for Setbacks

Understand that things might not always go smoothly. A good plan helps you to get back on track when you encounter obstacles or challenges.

Take Consistent Steps Forward

Remember, progress is progress, no matter how small. Consistent steps, whether big or small, will add up over time and help you cover great distances in your journey.

The Bottom Line

"Always aim at something meaningful in your life. Without a target, you're likely to achieve nothing. With a clear goal and a plan to reach it, every step you take, no matter how small, moves you closer to a life of freedom and success."

"The beauty of life is, while we cannot undo what is done, we can see it, understand it, change and move on."

    – Kendrick Lamar

TIP 3: Choosing the Right Company

Friends: Choose Wisely

It's great to have friends and to be loyal to them, but when you're on probation, you need to be extra cautious. Your friends could unintentionally lead you to violate your probation or parole, especially if you join them in negative or illegal activities. This could land you back in jail/prison or worse. Remember, a true friend wouldn't encourage you to do anything that puts your future at risk. If your friends are pushing you toward illegal activities, it's time to reevaluate those friendships.

Family: Love, but Be Cautious

Family members can also lead you astray, even though you might trust and love them. If they are encouraging you to engage in activities that could violate your probation or parole, you need to distance yourself from those situations. Love for family is important, but so is your future. If you find yourself struggling with family influences, seek guidance from a mentor or a trusted adult.

Romantic Relationships: Are They Supportive?

If you're in a relationship with someone who urges you to participate in negative activities, use drugs, or commit crimes, be very cautious. Your partner might not be on probation or parole and, therefore, might not understand the restrictions you face. They might invite you to nightclubs or parties, which could be risky for you. If the person you're dating isn't encouraging positive behavior and supporting your efforts to complete probation or parole, they may not be the right partner for you. A supportive partner should motivate and inspire you to stay on track.

Evaluating Your Circle: Are They Helping or Hindering?

Ask yourself: Are my friends, family, or partners genuinely supporting my efforts to complete probation or parole? Do they encourage positive actions, or do they lead me toward potential violations? If they're not positively influencing you, it's crucial to question their role in your life. Surround yourself with people who uplift and support your journey to complete probation and parole successfully.

The Bottom Line: Surround Yourself with Positivity

The people you spend time with can significantly impact your ability to complete probation or parole successfully. Choose to be around those who understand your situation and are committed to helping you succeed. Remember, your future is influenced by the choices you make and the company you keep.

"The art of moving forward lies in understanding what to leave behind."
– Andre 3000

TIP 4: Embrace Education as a Positive Outlet

School might not be everyone's favorite place. I understand that. Growing up, I didn't connect much with school either. But here's the thing: school is a valuable tool, especially when you're on probation. It helps fill your time with something constructive. If you haven't finished high school, now is the perfect chance to get that diploma or GED. Remember, many jobs and better-paying opportunities require at least a high school education.

Avoid Idle Time

Remember the saying: "Idle time is the devil's playground." It means that when you're not busy with productive activities, you're more likely to get drawn into trouble. Hanging out on the streets with friends who aren't into positive activities can lead to situations that might violate your probation. Keeping busy with schoolwork and classes reduces the time you spend in potentially risky environments.

Consider Community College as a Next Step

Already have your high school diploma or GED? Great! Now, think about enrolling in community college. You might not be a fan of formal education, but community college offers a wide variety of courses that could catch your interest. From basketball to sound engineering for aspiring rappers, graphic design, fashion, photography, and videography—there's something for everyone. Plus, financial aid can help pay for these classes, and you might even earn a little money while learning.

Education as a Probation Strategy

Staying engaged in school can significantly benefit you during probation or parole. It keeps your probation or parole officer informed about your positive steps and can be a strong point in your favor if you ever find yourself in court for a minor infraction. Demonstrating that you're actively pursuing education can be like an insurance policy for staying out of jail. I've seen many young people avoid incarceration because they were making progress in school.

The Takeaway: Use Education to Your Advantage

Don't underestimate the power of education during your probation period. It's not just about getting a diploma or learning new skills—it's about showing that you're working toward a better future. This approach can keep you on track, make a positive impression on your probation officer, and provide a solid defense in court if needed.

"Life is a movie, but there will never be a sequel."

– Nicki Minaj

TIP 5: Say No to Drugs

One of the most common reasons people on probation and parole get into trouble is through drug use. It might be cocaine, it might be weed, whatever it is—it's a huge risk. If you feel like you can't go without drugs during your probation, it's a sign of a deeper problem that needs attention. Your best bet is to stay off drugs completely for life. There's nothing good that comes from using drugs. Remember, drugs aren't going anywhere—they'll still be around after your probation or parole. Your main goal now should be to stay clean. Why risk having a positive drug test (a "dirty P test") that could lengthen your probation, send you back to jail, or even get you locked up for the first time?

The Deadly Game of Fentanyl

There's a drug called "fentanyl" out there—it's extremely dangerous. People mix it with other drugs and even make fake Percocet and Xanax pills with it. Fentanyl is so potent that even a tiny amount can be deadly. I've lost 24 friends to fentanyl in just two years. This isn't something to take lightly. If you didn't have a reason to avoid drugs before, let this be it. Your life is worth more than taking such risks.

Weed: A Long-lasting Trace

Weed stays in your system longer than most drugs. I'm not just saying this as an outsider; I've been on both federal and state probation and messed up because of weed. I even got caught right after smoking once. Don't fool yourself into thinking you can cheat the system with tricks to pass drug tests. Probation officers know these tricks too.

Substance Use Alters Your Mind

Even if you think you can handle it, substances change the way you think. You might think you're in control, but no one is the same when they're under the influence of drugs or alcohol. These substances can make you act out, get into fights, or do things you wouldn't normally do—all of which can land you back in jail or extend your probation. Worst case, you might end up facing new charges.

The Bottom Line: Just Say No

It's not worth playing with your future. Probation is a chance to move past mistakes, not make new ones. Stay away from substances, focus on your goals, and you'll get through this successfully.

"Don't worry about being a star, worry about doing good work, and all that will come to you."
– Ice Cube

TIP 6: Employment During Probation

Find a Job—Any Job

Getting a job is crucial. It doesn't matter if it's at McDonald's flipping burgers or stocking shelves at Walmart. The key is to get employed. A job keeps you busy and off the streets, reducing the chances of violating your probation or getting into new trouble. Being at work means you're staying out of situations that could jeopardize your freedom.

Earning Money

Having a job means having some money in your pocket. Sure, it might not be as much as you want or as much as you used to earn, but it's a start. Every bit helps, and having your own resources is important. If you are 18 years of age, consider looking into jobs in the construction and building trades. Many of these offer apprenticeship programs that don't require previous experience or higher education. Best of all, they often start with excellent pay and teach you skills and trades that you can use for life and potentially even start your own business with.

A Job as a Positive Activity

Working not only helps you pass the time during probation but also provides a convenient excuse to avoid risky invitations from friends. When you're invited to hang out in places or situations that might lead to trouble, being able to say, "Sorry, I have to work," is a valid and responsible response. Don't worry if your friends make fun of you for working—you're on a mission to complete your probation successfully.

Choose a Job in an Area You Like

If possible, find employment in a field that interests you. For example, if you're interested in becoming a barber, try to get a job in a barbershop, even if it's just cleaning or managing their social media. If music is your passion, look for opportunities in a studio or as an assistant to a producer. Being in an environment related to your interests can be extra motivating and educational.

Think Long-Term and Be Responsible

Remember, just because it's not your "dream job" doesn't mean you'll be stuck there forever. This is just a step to get you moving in the right direction. Don't settle for where you are now. Keep your eyes on the road ahead and stay on course. Also, don't quit a job before you have another one lined up. Be responsible at your workplace to avoid losing your job for reasons that can be avoided, such as being late, having a bad attitude, or missing days. Remember, your goal is to successfully complete your probation and build a foundation for your future.

The Bottom Line: Employment is Key

Having a job during your probation period is about more than just earning money. It's about staying focused, avoiding negative influences, and laying the groundwork for a better future. Every step you take now toward being responsible and committed contributes to your success. Additionally, having a job can help keep your probation officer off your back. Remember to maintain a good relationship with your boss or manager. A reference letter from them could be invaluable both during your probation and when it's time to seek another job.

"Dreams don't have deadlines. Believe in yourself."
– LL Cool J

TIP 7: Staying Off the Streets, Safe and Focused

Avoiding Street Influences

If you're serious about completing your probation or parole, it's crucial to stay off the streets as much as you can. There are people out there who might not think like you, who might provoke you into reacting in a way that could get you back on probation. Limit your outdoor activities to essential tasks like going to work, school, or other productive activities.

Law Enforcement and Probation

Even if you're not doing anything wrong, just hanging out on the streets can attract unwanted attention from law enforcement. For many on probation or parole, any police contact, even without an arrest, can be a problem. Such encounters can be used against you in court, often without a chance for you to explain. The best strategy is to minimize your presence on the streets.

Focusing on What's Important

It's not about giving up on life; it's about avoiding setbacks. Think about the times you were locked up or the possibility of being locked up again. Everything you think you're missing out on now will still be there after you complete your probation or parole, without the risk of violating it.

Dealing with Loss and Grief

Attending events like candlelight vigils or funerals, especially for those who lost their lives in gang-related incidents, can be risky. These events often attract police attention and could lead to violations, especially if you're associating with gang members or if someone you're with has illegal items like guns or drugs. It's safer to mourn privately or hold a small, personal remembrance at home. If you must attend a public service, go alone and avoid going with friends who might be carrying weapons or who are also under probation restrictions.

Self-Reflection and Decision-Making

Sometimes the risk doesn't come from others but from your own choices. If you feel the need to carry a weapon to an event, it's a clear sign that you shouldn't be going there. Getting caught with a weapon can lead to probation or parole violations and new charges. Always evaluate the necessity and safety of attending any event.

The Bottom Line: Prioritize Your Safety and Future

Remember, your primary goal is to complete your probation and build a better future. Making smart choices about where you go and who you associate with is crucial. Stay focused on positive activities and environments that support your journey toward a successful and free life.

"Did you hear about the rose that grew from a crack in the concrete? Proving nature's law is wrong, it learned to walk without having feet."

          – Tupac Shakur

Why It's Important to Stay on Track

Think Back to Being Locked Up

If you've been in jail before, try to remember what it was like. Think about having to share a tiny bathroom with someone else, always there, right next to you. Remember needing special shoes for the shower to avoid gross stuff like fungus, and always having to be on guard.

How You Were Treated and Feeling Alone

Think about how the guards treated you, which wasn't always nice. Remember how much you hoped for mail from friends or family, and how sad it was when no letters came. Missing your family and not being able to see them unless they came to visit you was really hard, wasn't it?

Dealing with Jail Rules & Politics

Remember all the rules and the way people acted in jail that you just had to go along with, even if you didn't want to. It's a part of jail life that makes it even tougher.

Jail Isn't Cool

Some people might act like being in jail is okay or even cool, but it's really not. It's tough, and it's not a good place for anyone. So, when you're making choices while you're on probation, think about all this stuff. And if you've never been to jail, trust me, you don't want to find out how bad it can be.

Make Smart Choices

As you go through your probation, keep all these memories in your mind. They can remind you why you're working hard to stay out of trouble. Your choices right now can help you avoid going back to a place that's tough and no fun. Stay on the right path so you can have a better future, one where you're free and can do things that make you happy and successful.

"My message is that you can do anything if you just believe."

      – Kanye West

What is Your Why?

Understanding your motivation for completing probation can be a powerful tool in staying focused and committed. This worksheet is designed to help you explore your personal reasons and the positive impacts of successfully completing your probation or parole.

Part 1: Why Do I Want to Complete Probation or Parole?

Take a moment to reflect on your personal reasons for wanting to complete your probation. Think about what drives you and write down your thoughts.

My Main Reasons for Completing Probation:
- Reason 1:
- Reason 2:
- Reason 3:

How Will Completing Probation Improve My Life?
- Short-Term Benefits:
- Long-Term Benefits:

What Positive Changes Do I Hope to See in Myself?
- Change 1:
- Change 2:
- Change 3:

Part 2: Who Would Be Happy If I Successfully Complete Probation or Parole?

Completing your probation isn't just about you. It also positively affects those around you. Think about the people who would be happy to see you succeed.

Family Members Who Would Benefit From My Success:
- Family Member 1:
- Family Member 2:
- Family Member 3:

Friends and Mentors Who Support Me:
- Friend/Mentor 1:
- Friend/Mentor 2:
- Friend/Mentor 3:

How My Success Would Affect Them:
- Effect on Person 1:
- Effect on Person 2:
- Effect on Person 3:

Part 3: Reflection

Take a moment to reflect on your answers. How does identifying your "why" make you feel about your journey through probation?

My Feelings After Completing This Worksheet:

One Action I Can Take Today Toward My Goal:

"Don't worry about what people say. Just focus on your goals and keep working."
— Nipsey Hussle

Goal Setting Worksheet: Proper Preparation Prevents a Poor Performance

Setting clear, achievable goals is crucial to successfully navigating through your probation or parole period. This worksheet is designed to help you identify your goals and create a plan to achieve them.

Purpose
To help you set and work toward clear, achievable goals during your probation period.

Part 1: Short-Term Goals
Short-term goals are milestones you can achieve in the near future. These should be specific, measurable, and achievable within a short timeframe.

Goal 1:
- Description:

- Deadline:

- Steps to Achieve:

Goal 2:
- Description:

- Deadline:

- Steps to Achieve:

Goal 3:
- Description:

- Deadline:

- Steps to Achieve:

Part 2: Long-Term Goals

Long-term goals are broader objectives you aim to accomplish over a longer period. They give direction to your life post-probation or parole.

Goal 1:
- Description:

- Timeframe:

- Steps to Achieve:

Goal 2:
- Description:

- Timeframe:

- Steps to Achieve:

Goal 3:
- Description:

- Timeframe:

- Steps to Achieve:

Part 3: Overcoming Obstacles

Identify potential challenges to achieving your goals and strategies to overcome them.

Obstacle 1:
- Description:

- Solutions/Strategies:

Obstacle 2:
- Description:

- Solutions/Strategies:

Obstacle 3:
- Description:

- Solutions/Strategies:

Part 4: Tracking and Reflecting

Keep track of your progress and reflect on your journey.

Progress Log:
- Date:
- Achievements/Progress:

Reflection:
- What have I learned?

- What adjustments do I need to make?

"No matter what happens, be grateful for every situation. It's all part of the journey."
– Meek Mill

Daily Schedule Planner
Worksheet Example

Effective time management is key to successfully navigating your probation period. This planner example will help you organize your daily activities, ensuring that your time is used wisely and productively.

Purpose

To help you plan and manage your daily activities, making sure that you allocate time effectively for school, work, appointments, and probation-related responsibilities.

How to Use

For each day, fill in the time slots with your planned activities, including school, work, any appointments, and important reminders for probation meetings or check-ins. This will help you stay organized and on track. Create one of these on a separate piece of paper weekly and use that to help stay on task.

Weekly Planner

Time/ Day	Mon	Tues	Wed	Thurs	Fri	Sat
6 AM						
7 AM						

8 AM						
9 AM						
10 AM						
11 AM						
12 PM						
1 PM						
2 PM						
3 PM						
4 PM						
5 PM						
6 PM						

7 PM					
8 PM					
9 PM					
10 PM					
11 PM					

Notes and Reminders

Use this space for any additional notes or important reminders for the week, such as probation meetings or special appointments.

This daily schedule planner will help you maintain a structured and balanced routine, ensuring all your essential commitments are met while also providing a clear overview of your week.

"Take advantage of the opportunities you have now because there isn't always a guarantee they'll be there tomorrow."
– Kendrick Lamar

Support Network Map
Worksheet

Building a solid support network is essential, especially during your probation period. This worksheet is designed to help you identify and organize the people and organizations that can offer you support.

Purpose

To help you recognize and connect with your personal support systems, including family, friends, mentors, and organizations that can assist you during your probation.

How to Use

List the individuals and organizations that make up your support network. Include their contact information and note how they can help you. This will help you know who to reach out to for different kinds of support.

Section 1: Supportive Individuals

Name	Relationship (e.g., Family, Friend, Mentor)	Contact Information	How They Can Help
Example: John Doe	Uncle	555-1234	Provides advice and emotional support

Section 2: Organizations & Systems

Organization Name	Type of Support (e.g., Educational, Legal)	Contact Information	How They Can Help
Example: ABC Youth Center	Mentorship Program	555-5678	Offers mentoring and after-school programs

Notes and Additional Contacts

Use this space for any additional notes, contacts, or important details about your support network.

This worksheet gives you a clear view of the people and organizations you can rely on for different kinds of support, making it easier to reach out when you need help.

"The only distinguishing factor between a winner and a loser is not quitting."

– Nipsey Hussle

Job Search Tracker
Worksheet

Staying organized during your job hunt is crucial. This worksheet is designed to help you keep track of the jobs you apply for, including important dates and contact information.

Purpose

To help you manage and monitor your job applications effectively, ensuring you stay organized and on top of your job search.

How to Use

List each job you apply for, noting the date of application, contact details of the employer, and any follow-up actions. This will help you keep track of where you've applied and the status of each application.

Job Application Log

Job Title/Position	Company Name	Date Applied	Contact Person	Contact Info	Status (e.g., Interviewed)	Notes/Follow-Up Actions
Example: Sales Assistant	ABC Retail	3/15/2024	Jane Doe	jane.doe@abcretail.com	Waiting for response	

Notes and Additional Details

Use this space for any additional notes about your job search, such as companies to research, job fairs to attend, or networking opportunities.

This job search tracker is a valuable tool for keeping your job applications organized and ensuring you follow up appropriately, maximizing your chances of finding suitable employment.

"Recognize and embrace your flaws so you can learn from them. Sometimes it takes a little polishing to truly shine."
– Kanye West

Community Service Log Worksheet

Keeping an accurate record of your community service is essential, especially when it's a requirement for your probation. This log will help you track your hours and the type of service you've completed.

Purpose

To document and monitor your community service hours, ensuring you meet any probation requirements related to community service.

How to Use

For each instance of community service you complete, log the date, the number of hours, the type of service, and get the signature of the supervising person. This will serve as a verified record of your participation and completion of service hours.

Community Service Record

Date	Hours Completed	Type of Service (e.g., Volunteering, Clean-up)	Supervising Person	Signature of Supervisor
Example: 04/10/2021	3	Park Clean-up	John Smith	[Signature]

Additional Notes

Use this space for any reflections on your community service experiences, skills learned, or any feedback received.

This community service log is a practical tool for keeping a clear and accountable record of your service hours, assisting in fulfilling your probation requirements effectively.

"Decide what to be and go be it."

        – Big Sean

Reflection Journal Pages Example

Journaling is a powerful tool for self-discovery and growth. This page is designed to help show you how to reflect on your daily or weekly experiences, challenges, achievements, and emotions.

Purpose

To provide a space for introspection and personal growth through regular journaling, helping you understand your journey better.

How to Use

Get a notebook or journal and use these prompts to guide your journaling. You can write daily or weekly, focusing on your challenges, achievements, feelings, and the lessons you're learning through your experiences.

Journal Prompts

Date:

Today's/This Week's Challenges:

Achievements I'm Proud Of:

How I Felt Today/This Week:

Lessons Learned:

Ways I Grew or Improved:

Something New I Tried or Experienced:

How I Handled Difficult Situations:

People Who Supported Me:

Things I'm Grateful For:

Goals for Tomorrow/Next Week:

Additional Thoughts and Reflections:

Notes:

- You can use your journal pages daily or weekly, depending on your preference.
- Feel free to add more to each section or create your own prompts.

"To appreciate the sun,
you gotta know what
rain is."
– J. Cole

Probation Compliance Checklist Worksheet

Staying on top of your probation requirements is crucial for successful completion. This checklist will help you remember and manage your probation terms, such as meetings, curfews, and drug tests.

Purpose

To assist in memorizing and fulfilling all your probation requirements, ensuring you remain compliant and on track.

How to Use

Use this checklist to note each requirement of your probation. Keep track of when these tasks must be done. This will help you stay organized and prevent forgotten obligations.

Probation or Parole Requirement Log

Probation or Parole Requirements (e.g., Meetings, Curfews, Drug Tests)	How Often	Time or Date	Notes
Example: Monthly Probation Officer Meeting	Once a month	3 pm on Thursdays	Met at probation office, discussed progress

Additional Notes

Use this space for any additional information, reminders, or details about your probation requirements.

This checklist is a practical tool for keeping a clear and organized record of your probation tasks, helping you meet your probation terms effectively and efficiently.

"Turn negative to
positive; life's what you
make it."
– Nas

Emergency Contacts
Worksheet

Having a list of emergency contacts is essential for quick access to help when needed. This worksheet allows you to organize and store crucial contact information.

Emergency Contact List

Contact Name	Relationship (e.g., Family, Probation Officer)	Phone Number	Email Address	Address (if applicable)	Notes (e.g., Best Time to Call)
Example: Jane Smith	Aunt	555-123-4567	jane.smith@email.com	123 Oak Street, Springfield	Call any time for urgent matters

Local Emergency Services

Service Type	Contact Name/Department	Phone Number	Address	Notes
Example: Hospital	Springfield Medical Hospital	555-911-9111	456 Elm Street, Springfield	Non-emergency number: 555-101-2021

Additional Notes

Use this space for any extra information or specific instructions related to your emergency contacts.

This emergency contacts worksheet is a vital tool for ensuring you have quick access to support in urgent situations, keeping you prepared and secure.

Walk With Me Impact: Further Info

Walk With Me Impact Media & Education is committed to innovating and providing impactful tools and training programs designed for at-risk populations and the dedicated individuals working with them. Our diverse array of educational materials and specialized trainings is specifically tailored to enhance your educational programs, thereby elevating their effectiveness and reach.

Central to our mission is tackling critical societal issues with practical and insightful strategies. Our focus areas include raising awareness about the dangers of Fentanyl, combating human sex trafficking, preventing gun violence, mitigating gang involvement, addressing substance abuse, and, importantly, working toward stopping recidivism. By providing resources that support rehabilitation and reintegration, we aim to break the cycle of re-offending and foster a path to positive, sustainable life changes for individuals.

We invite you to connect with us to learn how our services can be integrated into your programs, helping to transform lives and create safer, more resilient communities. Join Walk With Me Impact Media & Education in our journey to make a lasting impact. Together, we can work toward a future where education, awareness, and support pave the way for reduced recidivism and empowered lives.

Contact us today to explore how we can collaborate for a greater cause.

Website: www.wwmimpact.com
Email: info@wwmimpact.com
Address: 3960 West Point Loma Blvd #343, San Diego, Ca 92110

For information about special discounts for bulk purchases please contact Walk With Me Impact via email at: info@wwmimpact.com

Hood Proverbz: Further Info

Hood Proverbz is on a mission to empower our "inner city" communities, primarily focusing on those reentering society from incarceration. In California alone, around 35,000 individuals are released annually, each carrying hopes of success. Yet, we recognize that enhancing their self-efficacy could significantly fortify their belief in their own success. John Maxwell's wisdom rings true here: "If you focus on goals, you may hit goals. If you focus on growth, you will grow and always hit goals." Many of the individuals we encounter have goals but often lack self-development goals, which are crucial for real growth.

At the forefront of innovation, Hood Proverbz crafts transformative tools and training programs specifically tailored for the currently and formerly incarcerated and those committed to supporting their journey. Our portfolio includes a diverse range of educational resources and specialized training, all designed to boost the effectiveness of rehabilitative programs.

Central to our ethos is a commitment to pragmatically address societal challenges. We focus on personal growth, emotional intelligence, self-development, and instilling a firm belief in the potential for change. Our resources, aimed at supporting rehabilitation and reintegration, strive to break the cycle of re-offending and create a pathway to positive, sustainable changes in individuals' lives.

We go beyond addressing just the tangible needs. Hood Proverbz incorporates character development workshops, emotional intelligence classes, and goal-setting and execution webinars, all crafted and taught by experts with lived experiences. As Wayne Dyer insightfully said, "If we change the way we look at things, the things we look at change." This philosophy guides our approach to transforming how we assist, thereby revolutionizing the impact of our help.

We invite you to join us in this transformative journey. Discover how our services can integrate into your programs, igniting significant change and helping to build safer, more resilient communities.

Join Hood Proverbz in our pursuit of lasting change. Together, we can create a future where education, awareness, and unwavering support are the foundations for reducing recidivism and empowering lives.

Contact us today to explore how we can collaborate on this impactful and transformative cause. Together, let's change the way we look at helping, and in turn, change the lives we touch.

Website: www.hoodproverbz.com
Email: jonasroyster@hoodproverbz.com

www.ingramcontent.com/pod-product-compliance
Lightning Source LLC
Chambersburg PA
CBHW060324130626
46553CB00003B/906